Whispers In Verse

Maira Ahmed

BookLeaf Publishing

India | USA | UK

Presentation by *BookLeaf Publishing*

Web: www.bookleafpub.com

E-mail: info@bookleafpub.com

ISBN: 9789363304451

First edition 2024

*To my dadi & dada who loved telling me
stories.*

Calm in the Chaos

You feel the wind on your skin
On every fibre and inch
Before the rain falls
Before a thunderstorm

Trees sway as if hearing music
Puddles form like lyrics
Dark clouds fog the sky
The sweet smell of rain says hi

You smell it all
They call it *petrichor*
It's earthy and unique
Something you then constantly seek

And that's when you feel at peace
As the world crumbles, at your feet

The Passage of Time

As I look back and consider the days
I realise how much of it is a haze
The people I have met, the friends I made
Memories I would never want to trade
It all passed by in the blink of an eye
Now I'm wondering: did I even try?
To sit and enjoy the current moment
To maybe appreciate the present
Or the little things that make up my day
Like the dandelions that outline the bay
Like the autumn leaves in October,
As we grow older, we grow more sober
Then we understand the passage of time

Better In Stereo

In laughter's echos and silent tears
Through fleeting moments and the passing years
They stand by you through the darkest of days
And share the brightest summer days

When shadows fall and light begins to fade
A friend's embrace becomes a tiny shade
Their job being not only to protect and comfort
But to inspire and put in effort

They can be across an iPhone screen
But they'll always make you feel seen
Loyal to a fault
Keep your secrets safe like money in a vault

One minute you can go crazy
Screaming songs and dancing strangely
The next you're having deep talks
And you never want to stop

Echoes of a Sleeping Mind

In dreams we are the artists
Constructing the most vivid pictures
With paint and colour mixtures
Envisioning everything we wanted & wished

We change the past and act like it'll forever last
They have to be perfect, not a single mistake
Totally forgetting the fact—it's all fake
In truth, they go by so fast

The moment where we shut down and rest
It's an escape from reality
Essential for all of humanity
A place where no one can be stressed

Yet we avoid sleep
Because not all dreams are good, it seems

The Endless Cycle

When we are young, our hearts brightly blaze,
Running around with fierce and untamed fire,
Yet as we age, the light begins to haze,
Our dreams and passions become a maze

To social norms and values, we confine
We succumb to popular opinions
Choosing a more logical, safer line
Our only concern being to earn millions

Pressure from our parents
Pressure from our friends
Pressure from the random people across the
fence
This pressure never ends

And then when we retire
There is still so much we desire

Little Things

Watching a movie with my mother
Late-night talks with my brother
A walk in the evening
Spending all day daydreaming

My dad hugging me when I'm sad
Writing random stuff in a notepad
Warm hot chocolate with smores
Playing taboo and keeping meticulous scores

Little things make up your day
Almost like your day is on replay
Except you don't recognise it
Until it all goes to dirt

Free

What does it mean to be free?
It is a big wonder to me
Can you only breathe when you're underwater?
Or something else makes you feel like you
matter?

Is it looking up at a bright blue sky?
Or when you let the tears fall from your eye?
Does helping others make you smile?
Maybe it's something about your lifestyle?

For me, it's the green trees
And the big seas
So vast and free
Reminding me of how much there is left to see

The Whisper

I hear the faint whisper
It's barely a soft, husky murmur
And then came another
This time the voice was thicker

Each time, it became more urgent
Urging me to follow
Making me feel hollow
The current becomes emergent

It pushes and pulls
Prokes and prods
Leading me closer and closer to being
brainwashed
And I feel the allure

Hope

It's believing in yourself
When no one else does
It's putting the negative on a shelf
Caring about the present, not the *was*

It's putting yourself out there
Even when you're scared
Even though you have nothing left to care
To go out there and earn some respect

It's standing up for what you believe in
Chasing your dreams, not your demons
Doing everything you can to win
Always remembering your reason

It's having a goal in your mind
Knowing where you want to land
And when things knock you down in life
All that matters is you stand

Death

The fear of death is common
The uncertainty of the afterlife terrifying
Yet it's the only ending for a human
Every single one of us knows it's coming

You can go in your sleep
Or behind the wheel of a car
It can simply be what you eat
Or because you drank too much at that bar

But I can't help but wonder
Whether the one that dies is unlucky
Or the loved ones left behind to falter
Cursing light and anything funny

They have no laughter left
No one to answer their questions
All they can do is try their best
To maybe learn a lesson

The Office

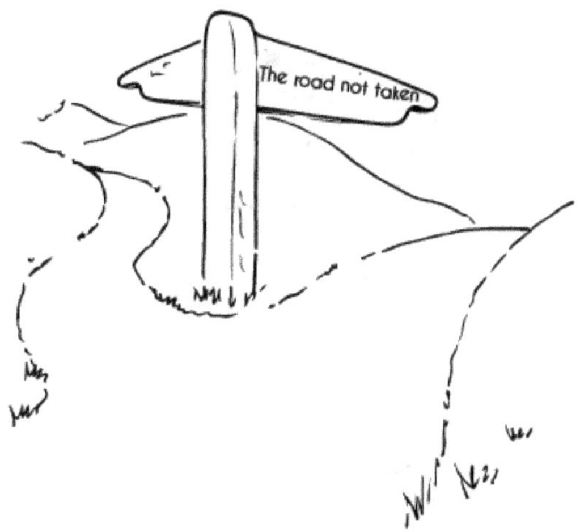

He bought her a duck
This other one got a second chance
While her true love wouldn't speak up
And the opportunities went by in a glance

She wanted to confess
But her friend didn't listen
Soon there were too many issues to address
And they soon lost their rhythm

We let things fester
Leaving us feeling guilty and heavy
Saying we don't want to hurt the other
But at the end of it, everyone just feels empty

Dadi

My grandma and brother used to play Ludo
She hated losing—a trait I inherited
She'd often stare out the window
But telling stories got her excited

When my parents put me in a crib
She got upset, saying, "She'll sleep with me
instead"
She loved chocolate
There is so much that I regret

I stayed in my room
To watch TV or read a book
I thought I had much more time, I assume
It was an idea I greatly mistook

Death Part 2

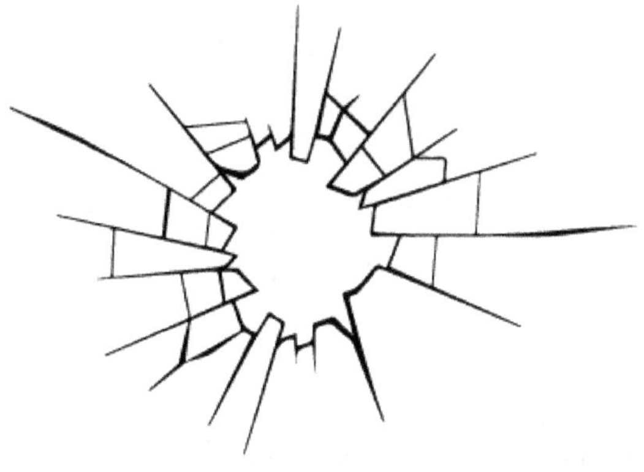

The shadow overcomes me
Yet, I'm not ready
There is no guarantee
That it won't be just empty

The sun has to set
But I'm grateful
For the love I've felt
For the people I've met, I'm thankful

It's better to go with no regrets
Embracing the fear and pain
Remembering to watch the sunset
With a smile on your face

The Coral Reefs

I remember being packed in gear
But feeling as light as a feather
There were people near
But all I remember is the bliss of the water
pressure

The reefs were beautiful
Must have seen a million different types of fish
All roaming around in little huddles
At that moment everything sailed into the abyss

I could've stayed forever
Observing and swimming silently
I knew I couldn't, however
Eventually I had to go back to a place not so
lovely

Dopamine

It's a funny thing—
How much people procrastinate
We delay and delay the starting
Knowing we'll never finish at this rate

We refuse to acknowledge what's important
Instead filling our time ranting about it
We don't want to waste a single moment
No matter the task is simple or unbearably
complicated

Our brains addicted to dopamine
Constantly taking up content after content
This generation never sees the sunshine
We're more obsessed with the prospect of a
comment

Heart

Friendship is supposed to come from the heart
Truth is it requires you to work hard
Filled with compromises and arguments
Containing both happy and sad moments

One second, making happy memories
The next second, the sky is filled with screams
As you age, time becomes less guaranteed
Suddenly everything has to compete

If you don't make the effort, it fizzles
Eventually it ends up becoming personal
You're making each other miserable
But letting go is a bigger struggle

But deep down inside I end up knowing
All we can do is continue hoping

In the World of Words

It's an entirely different world
Filled with entirely made-up characters
It's living in your dreamworld
Or imagining one that is much darker

It may be happy, it may be sad
It may be new, it may be one that's been there
for ages
You end up feeling grand
Every time you open those paper-filled pages

The ending may not be happy
No matter how much you wish it to be
It may make you bawl like a baby
It may make you scream, "Really?"

The best feeling is when you can't put it down
Turning page after page, reading word after
word
Having several meltdowns
Simple sentences that hurt

You're a part of something bigger
You're rooting for someone better
Small things acting as triggers
Every emotion trapped under this glamour

You feel the bitter, the baffled, the betrayal
You feel the calm, the cheerful, the confident
You feel the desperation, the despair, the dismay
Most of all, you feel something other than
vacant

Her Hair

He said she has the most beautiful face
He said he constantly thinks about her
In truth, she has got him in quite a haze
When he's looking at her, it's all a blur

Her hair smells alluring like lavender
That's how she caught his sight on the first day
She sat on the train and gained a stalker
Who fantasised about her all the way

And when they finally got off the train
He took a knife to her neck, she was dead
Bystanders tried to intervene in vain
The sirens came but the man never fled

Instead he took some of her pretty hair
Giving him something left of her to stare

The Sailor

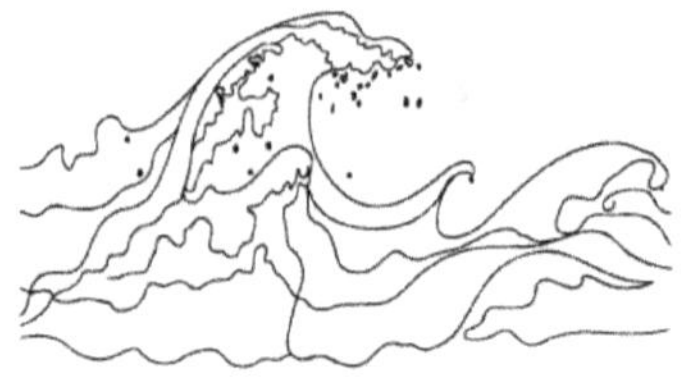

The wind in my hair
The gust on the sail
Not a single care
Ready to just bail

They say it's bad to run away
Yet I don't feel bad
As I make my getaway
Because there's absolutely no reason I'd come
back

It is beyond liberating,
The calming call of the ocean,
The soft sound of the waves churning
There is just something about the lack of
salvation

They say it's lonely out at sea
But how can I feel alone?
The birds are in the sky, carefree
And out here, I'm just unknown

Appreciation

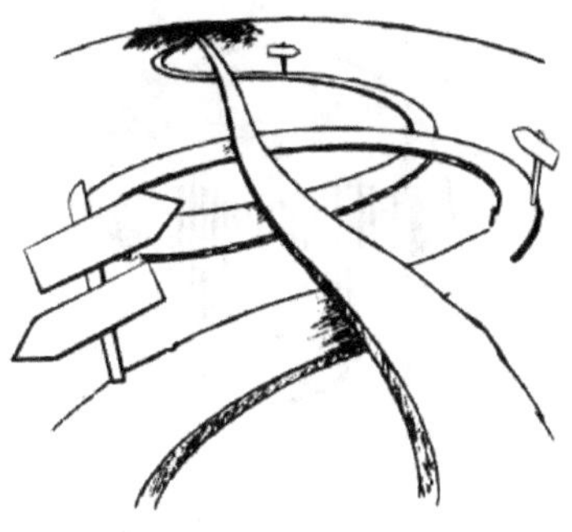

We're laughing, we're crying
We're singing, we're dancing
We're giving, we're fighting
We're listening, we're talking

We're watching a movie
We're buying jewellery
We're learning weird history
We're in the jacuzzi

We're growing up
We're learning to standup
We're going to a nightclub
We're taking the shortcut

We're passing by each moment
And soon it's all irrelevant

Marvellous Melodies

It's a plane that can take you anywhere
A way to travel everywhere
A combination of cultures
So much there to wonder

It can make you question everything
Or appreciate the little things
The sound absolutely beautiful
But sometimes the lyrics are just so soulful

It's full of melodies and harmonies
Yet, it's something you can't really study
There's a specific rhythm
However there is so much wisdom

It may make you cry
Or feel as peaceful as a bonsai
But it has that deep ability to manipulate
Just because it is so intimate

Love Story

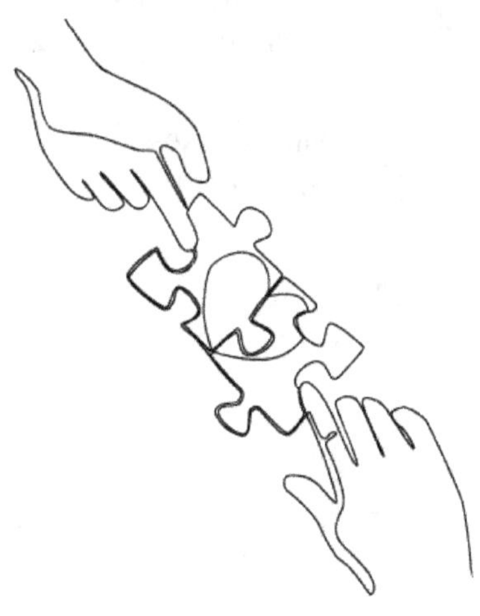

I can see us in the far future
With 2 kids running 'round the furniture
One of those large patios outside
Us simply looking on with pride

And I know you don't notice me
'Cause you talk about her incessantly
But is it too much to ask,
For you to just give me a glance

To you, we aren't even fathomable
But living without you seems unimaginable
I wait seconds, minutes, hours, days
And when you finally text it's all a haze

You ain't no Romeo, I ain't no Juliet
But there's no reason not to play this game of
roulette
We don't need to run away together
Or kill ourselves for each other

But if you want to try
I won't object to calling you mine

Brother

We fight about everything, from the colour of
spring to the height of the ceiling
We go from simple teasing to all-out screaming
You never miss a chance to annoy me
But being your sister is an honour of the highest
degree

I've shared every experience with you
Yet, somehow we've never gone to the zoo?
Remember when the scuba diving instructor had
to push me
It's fine though, 'cause you took 30 minutes to
learn how to breathe

Our relationship has evolved
From Nerf gun wars to deep talks
You're funny with a heart of gold
And I've never met someone as bold

You've always been my hero
Even though you're a big weirdo
Instead of being overprotective
You taught me how to have my own perspective

You help me figure out right from wrong
You taught me how to be strong
We're like two sides of a coin
Different, but still always joined

When I'm down, I know who to call
You're always there to catch me when I fall

Lost

I'm trapped in an empty box
The walls are suffocating, unforgiving
There is no key or lock
But I know there's no escaping

There are people around
They don't care, they don't notice
The walls won't break down
I'm delirious, losing focus

I scream again, trying to break out
It's like I'm drowning, no one can hear me
Nobody is waiting for me to reach out
I don't have anywhere to be

I shut down, silent as a spy
Inside, I shout loud
But I'm disconnected from the local WiFi
Nobody's coming, they're all lost in the clouds

I close my eyes
No one says goodbye

State of the World

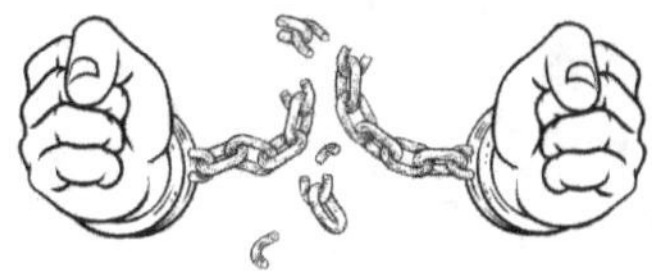

Why do we always have to be right?
Putting things out of mind, out of sight
We're obsessed with social etiquette
And god knows we hate being inadequate

The theme of love is constantly emphasised
So why does it make people feel compromised?
Hate is unbelievably prominent
Because we have a need to be dominant

We criticise doing bad things for good reasons
But applaud doing the right thing for the wrong
reasons
We hate each other without giving the other a
chance
We give them a glance but we're stuck in this
trance
The future is filled with possibilities
But just as many uncertainties
Either we're hung up on the bad
Or we refuse to believe in anything sad

There is no harmony here, no community
Just constant hostility or inequality

www.ingramcontent.com/pod-product-compliance
Lightning Source LLC
LaVergne TN
LVHW010256210726
843508LV00020B/2793